A Little Scottish Cookbook

Paul Harris

ILLUSTRATED BY KAREN

Also by Paul Harris:

Cooking with Beer
The Best of Bangladesh

First published by The Appletree Press Ltd, 1988
Text © Paul Harris, 1988
Illustrations © Karen Bailey, 1988

British Library Cataloguing in Publication Data
Harris, Paul
A little scottish cookbook.
1. Food: Scottish dishes – Recipes
641.59411

ISBN 0-86281-204-6

First published in the United States in 1988
by Chronicle Books, One Hallidie Plaza,
San Francisco, CA 94102
ISBN 0 87701 560 0

Printed in the EEC and bound by
Hunter & Foulis Ltd, Edinburgh, Scotland

Introduction

This is by no means any sort of attempt at a complete survey of Scottish cuisine: other writers have attempted this at greater length and in more substantial volumes and for readers whose appetite is further stimulated there is a list of recommended reading at the back of this little book. Rather, this is a collection of some of my own favourite dishes which, in my view, are typical of the cuisine of Scotland.

Scotland is a vast larder with fish, fowl and game a-plenty and many of these recipes reflect the availability of venison, pheasant, grouse, salmon and other foods which may, by some people, be regarded as luxury foods. But this is balanced out by traditional recipes for soups, fish and meat dishes enjoyed by the fisher folk and crofters of Scotland for generations. Read and enjoy.

A note on measures

In Scotland, as in the rest of Britain, Imperial measures – pounds, pints, etc. – are most widely used although the dreaded metric measures – kilogrammes, litres, etc. – are now making incursions thanks to the efforts of the EEC and our European neighbours. Both types of measure are given in the recipes here and for American readers cups and spoons are indicated. Stick to one though – do not mix the three measures in any one recipe or culinary disaster is likely to result.

All recipes, unless otherwise stated, are for four people of normal appetite.

Porridge

'Oats, and grain, which in England is generally given to horses. . . in Scotland supports the people'

Dr Johnson

Few would argue with Robbie Burns that porridge is 'Chief o' Scotia's food'. There are two important things to remember: always refer to porridge in the plural as 'them' and eat them standing up. Also soak overnight for best results.

---

1 pt/600 ml/2 cups water
2 oz/50 g/¼ cup oatmeal
1 level tsp salt

Boil water, add salt, sprinkle in oatmeal, stirring. Boil and place lid on pan. Simmer for 30 to 40 minutes, stirring frequently. If coarse oatmeal is used allow extra cooking time.

Soak overnight to reduce cooking time.

Herrings in Oatmeal

The staple diet of many Scots for centuries, the herring is a popular breakfast dish. Split before curing they are known as kippers.

---

4 herrings (cleaned)
4 oz/100 g/⅔ cup medium oatmeal
2 tsp salt
pinch of pepper
fat for frying

Bone the fish. Mix the salt and pepper with the oatmeal and coat each herring on both sides. Press the seasoned oatmeal mixture firmly into the fish.

Heat a little fat in the frying pan. Fry over a medium heat until lightly brown on one side, then turn over and cook the other side (approximately 3 minutes per side).

Drain the fish. Serve with lemon and parsley.

Arbroath Smokies

These are small haddock, cleaned but not split open, salted, tied in pairs by the tails and then hung on wooden spits above a fire – preferably of oak or silver birch chips.

---

4 whole smoked haddock	salt and pepper
¾ pt/450 ml/1½ cups milk	butter

Separate the pairs of Arbroath smokies and lay them in a shallow dish. Pour on the milk and add salt and pepper. Spread on butter and cover with foil. Cook in a moderate oven (gas mark 4, 350°F, 180°C) for 25-30 minutes.

Aberdeen Butteries

Enjoyment of these is something of a matter of personal taste. It is said that Aberdeen fishermen used to take them out to sea: the fat content kept them warm in the North Sea. There are precious few fishermen left today, so it is difficult to establish the veracity of this.

This recipe makes approximately two dozen.

---

1 lb/450 g/3 cups flour
1 oz/25 g baker's yeast (½ tbsp dried yeast)
1 tbsp salt
½ pt/300 ml/1 cup lukewarm water
6 oz/175 g/⅔ cup lard
6 oz/175 g/⅔ cup butter or margarine
1 level tbsp caster sugar

Sieve the flour into warm mixing bowl. Mix yeast, salt and sugar and add to the flour along with the lukewarm water. Mix together and set in a reasonably warm place to rise. Keep covered with a warm damp towel while it proves.

Beat fats until blended, then divide into three equal parts. Roll out dough into a strip on a floured board. Fold in three and roll out flat as you would for flaky pastry.

Repeat twice. Divide into oval bun shapes.

Put apart on a greased and floured tray and prove in a warm place for another thirty minutes or so, then bake in a fairly hot oven (gas mark 6, 400°F, 200°C) for 20-25 minutes. Reduce the heat as the rolls cook.

Potted Hough

This is a tasty savoury dish, or you may prefer it as a starter. Potting is an ancient method of preserving food.

---

1 lb/450 g hough (shin of beef)
2 lb/900 g beef shin bone
1 tsp salt
6 allspice berries
6 peppercorns
1 small bay leaf
1 pinch paprika

Put the meat and bone into a pan and cover with cold water. Bring to the boil, and simmer for about 3 hours.

Cut the meat into small pieces. Remove meat from the bone. Return the bone to the pan, add salt, allspice berries, peppercorns, bay leaf and paprika and boil the liquid rapidly until it has reduced by about half. Put the meat into a large mould, pour in the stock and put in the fridge to set. Serve next day out of the mould, with a salad if desired.

Stovies

Simple but surprisingly delicious. The potatoes should be unblemished and of equal size. The name 'stovies' comes from the French 'étouffer', to stew in a closed vessel.

½ oz/15 g butter
2 thin slices bacon (chopped)
1 lb/450 g potatoes
1 large onion
½ pt/300 ml/1 cup hot water
salt and pepper

Melt the butter in a pan. Peel and slice the onion and fry in the butter with the bacon. Peel and slice the potatoes and add them to the pan. Season and add the water to a depth of ½ inch. Put the lid on the pan and cook slowly for 1-1½ hours. Stir as necessary to prevent the potatoes sticking to the pan.

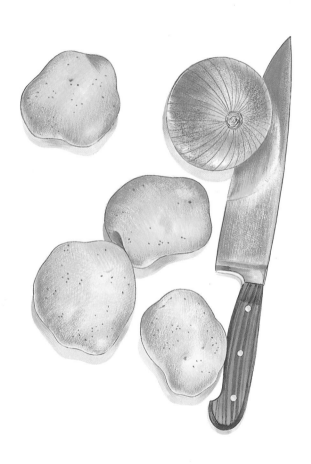

Scotch Woodcock

An easily made, mouth-watering, savoury dish.

½ oz/15 g butter	dash of tabasco sauce
1 tbsp milk	thinly sliced toast
1 egg	anchovy fillets
salt and pepper	capers
pinch of paprika	

Melt the butter, beat the egg, add milk and seasoning and scramble. Butter the toast, mound scrambled egg on top. Place an anchovy fillet across the egg and put a caper on either side.

Forfar Bridies

The individual steak pies from Forfar, Angus, were immortalised by J.M. Barrie in *Sentimental Tommy*. They are the Scottish equivalent to the Cornish pasty.

Filling	Pastry
1 lb/450 g chuck steak	1 lb/450 g/4 cups plain flour
3 oz/75 g/⅔ cup prepared shredded suet	pinch of salt
1 onion (finely chopped)	4 oz/100 g/½ cup margarine
salt and pepper	4 oz/100 g/½ cup lard

Sift the flour and salt together, add the lard and margarine

15

cut into pieces and rub in. Stir in enough cold water to make a stiff dough then turn it onto a floured surface; knead gently. Divide dough into four. Trim the steak, removing any excess fat, then pound it. Cut the meat into thin strips and mix it with the suet and onion and plenty of seasoning. Roll each piece of dough out to a 6 inch/15 cm round shape. Divide the filling among each and seal the edges well with water.

Make a hole in the centre of each bridie with a skewer and bake at gas mark 6, 400°F, 200°C for 20 minutes. Reduce the temperature to gas mark 4, 350°F, 180°C and bake for a further 35-45 minutes or until golden brown.

Serve hot with peas and potatoes.

Scots Mince

This wholesome Scottish family dish is sometimes known as 'Scotch Collops', from the French 'escalope', meaning thin slivers of meat. It is one of Scotland's most popular dishes to this day.

1 lb/450 g/2 cups best minced beef (firmly packed)	1/2 pt/300 ml/1 1/4 cups beef stock
1 medium onion (peeled and sliced)	2 bay leaves
	1 level tbsp oatmeal
salt and pepper	1/2 oz/15 g dripping

Melt the dripping in a pan, add the onion and fry it for a few minutes. Stir in the mince and brown it carefully, stirring constantly to avoid lumps. Mix in the salt, pepper and stock together with the oatmeal and bay leaves. Simmer for about 45 minutes or until the meat is cooked. Serve with mashed potatoes. Turnips ('neeps') are an optional extra vegetable.

Oatcakes

The ancient fourteenth-century chronicler, Froissart, records that the Scottish soldiers without fail carried a flat plate and a wallet of oatmeal. Using a little water, they were always able to make themselves an oatcake over an open fire.

If necessary, a heavy frying pan can be used instead of a girdle (or griddle as it is otherwise known). Heat before use. Here is Janet Murray's recipe.

1 lb/450 g/2 cups fine oatmeal	1 tbsp bicarbonate of soda
	1 tsp salt
1 tbsp liquid fat	boiling water

Good dripping or bacon fat is ideal for oatcakes, and must be melted before using. Put oatmeal into a bowl, add the salt and bicarbonate of soda, then pour in the fat and mix a little. Now quickly pour in enough boiling water to make a soft dough and roll into a lump.

Scatter more oatmeal over a baking board, and knead

the dough on it, working it to a smooth ball. Spread the dough out with the knuckles, sprinkling oatmeal over and under as required, then roll it out to about ⅛ inch/3 mm in thickness. Use the palm of the hand to rub off most of the oatmeal then brush it over.

Cut the cakes into triangles and bake on a fairly hot girdle, turning the cakes when they are brown. Finish off in front of the fire or in a hot oven.

Butterscotch

Those with a sweet tooth will enjoy the sweet and creamy taste of butterscotch. This recipe makes about 1 lb/450 g.

---

1 lb/450 g/2 cups soft brown sugar
½ lb/225 g/½ cup butter (creamed)
juice of 1 lemon

Dissolve the brown sugar in a pan. When it turns to liquid add the butter and the lemon. Allow to boil but stir gently the whole time for 15 minutes or so. The right consistency is achieved when, if a little is dropped into very cold water, it hardens.

Beat your mixture firmly for 5 minutes; pour onto a buttered tin and when it has cooled mark it into squares with a knife. When cold it will set hard. Tap the bottom of the tin with a rolling pin and it will break up into squares.

Instead of the lemon, some people prefer a ginger flavour and for this you should substitute a heaped teaspoon of ground ginger for the lemon.

Shortbread

In the past, shortbread was eaten particularly at Hogmanay or Christmas. Now it is, of course, taken through the year although it is directly descended from the old Yule bannock, notched around the edges to signify the rays of the sun.

---

4 oz/100 g/1 cup plain flour
2 oz/50 g/½ cup rice flour
4 oz/100 g/1 cup butter
2 oz/50 g/½ cup caster sugar

Sieve the flour and rice flour. Add the sugar and butter and mix together until the mixture resembles the consistency of shortcrust pastry. Form into a square cake and cut into fingers. Pinch the edges and prick all over with a fork.

Bake in a steady oven (gas mark 3, 325°F, 160°C) until beginning to colour, then lower the heat and bake for a further 45-60 minutes.

Cool on grill pan tray.

Cock~a~Leekie

This is probably Scotland's most famous soup and is often found on the menu at a Burns Supper or St Andrew's Night dinner. From the humblest crofts to the grandest of royal palaces this was an established favourite. Here is the special recipe of Rosa Mattravers, cook to Theodora, Lady Forbes, on Donside in Aberdeenshire.

---

1 boiling fowl
large veal or beef marrow bone (optional)
3 rashers lean bacon (chopped)
salt and pepper
12 leeks (chopped)
4 oz/100 g/1 cup cooked prunes
parsley, thyme and a bay leaf

Place chicken, bacon, chopped bones, herbs, and most of the leeks into a large saucepan and cover with water. Put the lid on and let it simmer for 2 to 3 hours, topping up with more water if necessary, until the bird is cooked.

Season to taste, then strain, picking out the chicken and cutting it into serving pieces and spooning out the marrow bones. Add these to the soup, together with the stoned prunes, and the remaining chopped leeks. Simmer gently for 10-15 minutes.

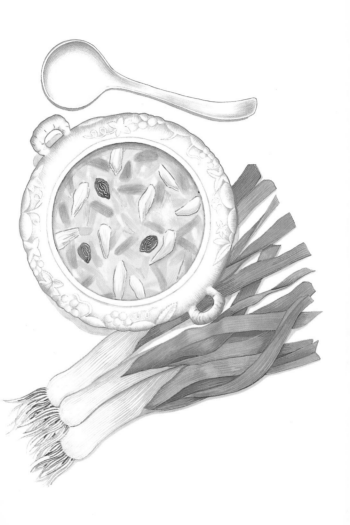

Partan Bree

'Partan' is the Scots word for crab and 'bree' means a liquid. This soup was traditionally a firm favourite with Scots fisher folk.

---

6 oz/175 g/¾ cup rice
1 pt/600 ml/2 cups milk
1 large boiled crab
1 pt/600 ml/2 cups white stock
dash/8 drops anchovy essence
dash/8 drops tabasco
pepper and salt
mace
¾ pt/450 ml/1½ cups thin cream
cayenne pepper to taste

Boil the rice in the milk until it becomes soft. Take the meat out of the crab and put to one side. Sieve the rice, milk and soft crab meat. Stir in stock, anchovy essence, tabasco and seasoning to taste. Bring gently to boil and add a pinch of mace and the cream. Garnish with flaked claw meat and cayenne pepper.

Cullen Skink

This is not an offensive small animal but a traditional recipe for soup from the Moray Firth area. 'Skink' comes from the Gaelic and means 'essence'.

1 large smoked or finnan haddock	½ oz/15 g/1 tbsp butter
1 chopped onion	salt and pepper
1½ pints/900 ml/3 cups milk	mace
	2 tbsp cream
mashed potatoes as needed	parsley

Skin the haddock and put into a shallow pan or casserole dish, and add just enough cold water to cover. Bring slowly to the boil. Simmer until the consistency of the haddock becomes creamy.

Remove from the pan and part the flesh from the bones. Break the fish into flakes. Return the bones to the water in the pan and add the onion. Cover and simmer gently for 20 minutes. Strain this stock.

Return stock to a clean pan and bring to the boil. In another pan bring the milk to the boil and add to the stock with the flaked fish. Simmer for three or four minutes but do not allow to stick to pan. Stir in hot mashed potatoes to make a creamy consistency. Add butter gradually and salt, pepper and mace to taste. Stir in the cream and, before serving, scatter the chopped parsley over the hot soup. Best served with finely sliced, dry toast.

Scotch Broth

Also known as barley broth, Boswell records that Dr Johnson was particularly rude about this nourishing soup:

'. . . you never ate it before?'

'No sir,' replied Johnson, 'but I don't care how soon I eat it again.'

(*Journal of a Tour to the Hebrides*, 1786)

---

1 lb/450 g neck of mutton (flank or shank), alternatively flank of hough of beef
2 pt/1 l./4 cups cold water
1 oz/25 g/1 tbsp barley
pepper and salt
1 medium turnip (diced)
1 leek
1½ oz/35 g/½ cup shelled peas
1 carrot (grated)
1 tsp minced parsley
small piece of cabbage (grated)

Put meat into a large pan with enough cold water to cover. Add salt and the well-washed barley. Bring to boiling point and skim. Add pepper, diced turnip, peas and leek. Simmer for one and a half hours. Half an hour before serving add the grated carrot and the cabbage.

When ready lift out the meat and cut into dice and return the flesh to the pan. Add the parsley and serve hot. Feel free to vary the vegetables according to whatever is in season.

Skye Prawns

The Skye prawn is otherwise known as a Dublin Bay prawn or langoustine. Although the following is not a traditional recipe this delicious sharp-tasting sauce provides the perfect accompaniment for the prawns.

---

1 lb/450 g king prawns
1 lemon
1/4 pt/150 ml/1/2 cup mayonnaise
2 tsp tomato puree
1 tbsp double cream
pinch of paprika
dash tabasco
pepper

Mix together mayonnaise, tomato puree, paprika and tabasco. Season to taste. Boil prawns in salted water for 2 minutes only. Remove and shell. Fold cream into sauce mixture and serve with prawns. Garnish with wedges of lemon and whole (unshelled) prawns.

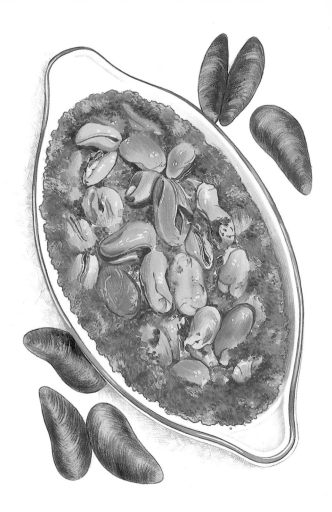

West Coast Mussels

Mussels from the sea lochs of the west coast are delicious. To prepare them, scrub clean and boil in water. Discard any of the shells which do not open. Highland hostess The Lady Glentruim serves these *par excellence* at Glentruim Castle in Inverness.

---

1 lb/450 g cooked mussels
4 oz/100 g/½ cup butter
2 oz/50 g/¼ cup breadcrumbs
4 tbsp white wine
1 small onion
½ clove garlic
salt and pepper

Fry breadcrumbs in half the butter and put to one side, then fry the chopped onion and garlic in the remaining butter. Put the mussels, onion, and garlic seasoning in a shallow dish and cover with wine and breadcrumbs. Heat in oven pre-set at gas mark 5, 375°F, 190°C for 10-15 minutes and serve piping hot.

Salmon Steaks

This king of fish requires very little in the way of addition or garnishing. Here is a simple recipe.

---

4 slices salmon (about ¾ in/2 cm thick)
salt and pepper
2 tbsp melted butter
parsley
lemon

Wipe the salmon slices with a damp cloth and brush over with melted butter. Season with salt and pepper on both sides. Place the slices under a hot grill. Grill each side for 5 minutes or so, as necessary. Serve garnished with parsley and sliced lemon.

Roast Pheasant

The hen is generally tastier than the better looking cock. The bird should be well hung: the traditional test was to hang by the tail and when the body fell to the cellar floor it was ready for the pot!

---

1 pheasant
small piece of butter
redcurrant jelly
1 orange
slices of fat bacon
1 small glass claret

Pluck and gut the pheasant (you'll need to look elsewhere for your instructions if tackling this for the first time!); put a piece of butter, some redcurrant jelly and an orange inside the body to keep it moist. Put slices of bacon on the breasts and place the pheasant on a rack over a tray in the oven.

Cook in a moderate oven for 45-60 minutes. Just before the bird is ready, baste it with the liquid in the tray. Return to the oven, set at gas mark 7, 435°F, 220°C, and leave till brown, about 10 minutes.

Place bird on serving dish. Strain fat from tray, leaving sediment. Add ½ pt cold water, skim off solidified fat; stir well, boil up on hot plate with claret and season. Serve with gravy, bread sauce and cranberry sauce or claret jelly.

Pigeon Casserole

In days of yore dovecotes were plentiful in town and country and pigeons were much favoured as a useful extra source of meat. They are a cheap and distinctively flavoursome and, cooked long and slow, are excellent as a casserole dish.

2 old pigeons	8 oz/200 g chopped
4 oz/100 g streaky bacon	mushrooms
1 oz/25 g/2 tbsp butter	1 tbsp browned flour
1 cup claret	salt and pepper
1/4 pint/150 ml/1/2 cup water	2 bay leaves
or stock	

Pluck and gut the birds. Wipe pigeons inside and out with a damp cloth. Chop bacon and fry in a shallow saucepan with a little butter. Add the pigeons and fry lightly for 5 minutes. Transfer contents of pan to a casserole dish.

Pour claret and stock into a pan. Add mushrooms, bay leaves and salt and pepper. Bring to the boil and reduce and thicken with the flour as necessary. Pour over the pigeons. Cover and cook in a slow oven, gas mark 5, 375°F, 190°C, until tender (1½ - 2 hours).

Grouse and Steak Pudding

Alas, now almost in the category of an endangered species, the Glorious Twelfth (of August) is no longer quite so glorious. The Red Scotch Grouse is reckoned by the *cognoscenti* to be the finest game bird in the world and now exists only in Scotland and some parts of the north of England. Hang for at least a week and roast the young birds; the older ones will make an excellent pudding.

1 old grouse	3-4 bay leaves
8 oz/250 g chuck steak	1/2 tsp thyme
1 small onion	1/2 tbsp powdered gelatine
1 clove	chopped parsley
celery	salt and pepper
1 carrot	shortcrust pastry

Bone the grouse. Make a stock with the bones, the vegetables, herbs and seasoning. Simmer for 3 hours. Add the gelatine and let cool. Slice the flesh off the grouse and cut up the meat. Season to taste.

Take a pie dish and put a layer of steak, then a layer of grouse, then a layer of onion and parsley. Finish with another layer of steak. Add half the stock and allow it to set.

Cover with pie dough, brush with egg yolk and cook for 3 hours: the oven should be hot to start with and when the pastry browns cover pie with greaseproof paper and reduce to medium oven. When cooked, add the balance of the stock through a hole in the top of the pie. Serve cold.

Haggis

Everybody knows that a haggis is a small, scruffy, hairy animal accustomed to running through hedges backwards. It is so elusive that you will have to make do with this recipe for what many would regard as Scotland's very own national dish, always served on Burns Night.

1 sheep's paunch (stomach bag)	nutmeg
heart, lung and liver of sheep	2 onions (chopped)
1 tsp salt	6 oz/175 g/1 ½ cups toasted oatmeal
black pepper, freshly ground	1 lb/450 g/4 cups beef suet
mace	¾ pt/450 ml/1 ½ cups stock

The following recipe is not for the weak of constitution! Wash the paunch well in cold water. Turn it inside out and scrape with a knife. Boil the heart, liver and lung until tender, hanging the windpipe out over the edge of the pan so that it drains into a bowl.

Chop the meat finely and grate the liver. Spread this out and add salt, pepper, mace, nutmeg, onions, suet and oatmeal. Mix well with stock and fill the paunch with the mixture. Leave some room for the oatmeal to swell in the cooking. Sew it up with a trussing needle and coarse thread or very fine string.

Prick all over with a needle and put into boiling water for 3 hours. Remove from the pan and place on a hotplate. Remove the threads, slit open the bag and serve steaming hot with mashed potatoes and mashed turnips ('chappit

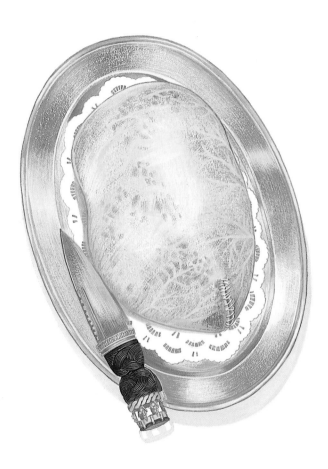

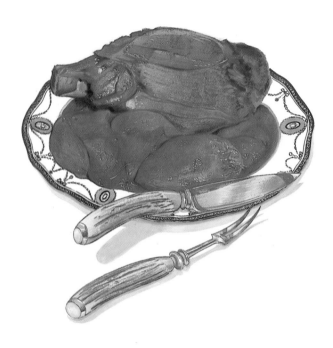

tatties' and 'bashed neeps'). Ensure suitable musical accompaniment is available (i.e. a kilted piper) before serving!

Roast Venison

Some of the finest venison in the world is to be found in Scotland where the deer roam free on the high mountain tops. This recipe is for roasting a large joint for serving with a traditional sauce.

I haunch of venison (about 6 lb/2½ kg)	**Sauce**
paste of flour and water	I glass port wine
salt and pepper	I tbsp redcurrant jelly
2 tbsp butter	kidneys from venison
I glass claret	I tbsp flour
flour	I tbsp butter

The venison should be well hung before cooking. Sponge it with warm water and rub over with butter. Cover with greaseproof paper and over this lay a paste of flour and water so that the surface is well covered. Wrap in foil and roast for around four hours at gas mark 3, 325°F, 160°C.

Remove foil and paper and test with fork. Season with salt and black pepper, dredge with flour, baste well with melted butter and claret and brown quickly. Serve with the hot sauce.

To make the sauce, lightly fry the venison kidneys in butter, remove them from the pan and add the port and seasoning to the pan juices. Reduce and thicken with flour as necessary. Add the redcurrant jelly and boil. Serve over the venison.

Venison should always be accompanied by a good Burgundy.

Clootie Dumpling

This pudding takes its name from the cloth, or clout, in which it is boiled.

6 oz/175 g butter	1 lb/450 g/1½ cups sultanas
12 oz/350 g/3 cups flour	8 oz/225 g/¾ cup currants
4 oz/100 g/1 cup sugar	1 tbsp treacle
1 tsp baking soda	1 tbsp syrup
1 tsp cinnamon	2 eggs (beaten)
1 tsp ginger	milk to mix

Rub butter into the dry ingredients. Make a well and add the syrup, treacle, beaten egg and enough milk to make a stiff mix. Prepare the pudding cloth by dipping it into boiling water and then dusting it generously with flour. Put the mix on the cloth and tie well with string, allowing a large enough pocket for the pudding to expand. Boil for 3 hours.

Atholl Brose Pudding

Originally served as a drink, with cream this can become a rich and delicious dessert, a sort of Scottish syllabub.

1/2 pt/300 ml/1 cup double cream
3 fl oz/75 ml/1/4 cup whisky
3 tbsp heather honey
2 oz/50 g/1/3 cup pinhead oatmeal (toasted)

Whip cream until firm. Stir in the oatmeal with the honey. Chill then, just before serving, mix in the whisky.

Scottish Cheeses

There are some delicious and distinctive Scottish cheeses of which these are my favourites.

Caboc has been made in the Highlands for more than 400 years and is quite the most distinctive. It is a rich, creamy cheese of soft consistency shaped like a croquette and rolled in oatmeal, which gives it a very special nutty taste.

Orkney is made in the islands to the north of the mainland from skimmed milk. It is like a mild Cheddar, and is available in red or white. The smoked ones have the best flavour.

Dunlop is similar to Cheddar, available in red or white and is named after a village in Ayrshire. A local woman who fled to Ireland to avoid religious persecution in the late seventeenth century, Barbara Gilmour, brought the recipe back with her. Soft with a mellow flavour.

Stewart Cheeses are a Scottish version of Stilton. They come in blue or white and are slightly milder than Stilton. The blue cheese is generally more popular, the white being rather salty.

Crowdie is a very old type of cheese traditionally made in the crofts of the Highlands. It is now available commercially, usually in cartons as it is a very soft cheese. It is made with milk fresh from the cow and, unusually, is only semi-cooked. Excellent with salads and on oatcakes and bannocks.

Dundee Cake

The almond-covered top of this cake is renowned at Scottish tea tables and is particularly popular at traditional events like christenings and birthdays.

6 oz/175 g/²/₃ cup butter	3 oz/75 g/¹/₂ cup raisins
6 oz/175 g/²/₃ cup caster sugar	3 oz/75 g/¹/₂ cup mixed peel
3 eggs	1 oz/25 g/1 tbsp ground almonds
9 oz/250 g/1 cup flour	3 oz/75 g/¹/₂ cup blanched almonds
¹/₂ tsp baking powder	milk
6 oz/175 g/²/₃ cup sultanas	
3 oz/75 g/¹/₂ cup currants	

No Dundonian connection is required to tackle this one – indeed, the origins of the name are lost in the mists of time.

Cream the fat and sugar. Add the eggs one at a time and beat well. Add the dry ingredients, prepared fruit, and the ground almonds. Add milk if necessary to make dropping consistency.

Put in a greased and lined tin and arrange blanched almonds on top to make a pattern. Bake at gas mark 4, 350°F, 180°C for 1½ hours.

Coffee with Drambuie

Drambuie is *the* liqueur of Scotland and has an ancient and honourable pedigree. Fleeing from the English forces, Bonnie Prince Charlie took refuge with the Mackinnons of Strathaird on Skye. As a gift for their hospitality, he gave them the recipe for his own liqueur. It is still made to this day from that secret recipe based, naturally, upon whisky. Coffee with Drambuie is delicious served at the end of a meal.

---

1 measure Drambuie
1-2 tsp soft brown sugar
pot of strong coffee
double cream

To make each serving take a stemmed glass and warm. Put in the Drambuie, stir in the brown sugar and fill with coffee to just an inch below the rim. Stir until the sugar is fully dissolved then pour on the cream over the back of a teaspoon, so that it floats on the surface.

Edinburgh Rock

Fergusons were the great Edinburgh rock makers and here is their secret, patent recipe for the sweet which has travelled the world.

---

1 lb/450 g/2 cups granulated or crushed lump sugar
³⁄₈ pt/200 ml/¾ cup water
½ tsp cream of tartar

Heat the sugar and water until the sugar is dissolved. When about to boil add the cream of tartar and boil without stirring until it reaches 250°F, 130°C, or until it forms a hard ball in cold water.

Take from the heat and add colouring as required. Remember the colour will fade as the candy is 'pulled'. Pour on to a buttered marble slab, or into buttered candy bars. Cool slightly and turn the edges to the centre with an oiled scraper, but do not stir.

When cool enough to handle, dust it with icing sugar, and 'pull' it evenly and quickly, taking care not to twist it, until it becomes opaque and dull. This should be done in a warm kitchen, or near a heater if the candy becomes stiff too quickly. Draw out the candy into strips and cut into short lengths with a pair of oiled scissors.

Leave in a warm room on greased paper for at least 24 hours, when the rock will become powdery and soft. It can be stored in an air-tight tin. If the candy remains sticky, it means that it has not been pulled enough.

Further Reading

Ena Baxter, *Ena Baxter's Scottish Cookbook*, Stirling, 1974.

Catherine Brown, *Scottish Regional Recipes*, Glasgow, 1981.

Theodora Fitzgibbon, *A Taste of Scotland*, London, 1970.

The Lady Glentruim, *Dinners in a Scottish Castle*, Edinburgh, 1983.

F. Marian McNeill, *The Book of Breakfasts*, Edinburgh, 1975.

F. Marian McNeill, *Recipes from Scotland*, Edinburgh, 1946.

F. Marian McNeill, *The Scots Kitchen*, Glasgow, 1925.

Janet Murray, *With A Fine Feeling for Food*, Aberdeen, 1972.

Queen's College, Glasgow, *The Glasgow Cookery Book*, Glasgow, 1975.

Janet Warren, *A Feast of Scotland*, London, 1979.

Molly Weir, *Molly Weir's Recipes*, Edinburgh, 1980.

Index